LEADERSHIP HAPPENS
WHEN YOU
MOVE

An Introduction
& Common Leadership Error

Dr. James A. Prokop

GLY Group

GLY Group

ISBN: 979-8-218-97407-7

Library of Congress Control Number: 2024905127

PRINTED IN THE UNITED STATES OF AMERICA

To my eternal love, Andrea.
&
Those family and rare friends who change our lives forever.

In him, all things are possible.

A million Little Miracles.

The Why

At the beginning of my leadership journey, I would miss the simple things like walking down an office hallway and asking a team member to meet me in my office with no context or expectations as an issue. This simple interaction could lead to a moment of concern or strife for that individual. The team member's mind can quickly become a breeding ground for uncertainty and anxiety. Without any information about the purpose of the meeting or what might be expected of them, various thoughts and worries may flood their consciousness. They might question whether they made a mistake, if their performance is being criticized, or if they are in trouble. The lack of context leaves room for their imagination to create worst-case scenarios. This uncertainty can erode their confidence and create unnecessary stress, leading to a moment of concern or even potential strife. Additionally, this situation can also trigger interpersonal dynamics within the team. Other members of the team may wonder why they were specifically not chosen, leading to feelings of favoritism or exclusion among their colleagues. Current and future leaders should have a basic understanding of the impacts of small interactions with others.

This text attempts to create a foundational understanding of leadership, the leader's interactions with the followers around them, recognizing a common error while applying a perspective of a relatively new leadership theory to avoid the errors and improve as a leader. The next step in this journey is a detailed application of this new approach to leadership theory with real-world examples.

LEADERSHIP

MANY SCHOLARLY BOOKS, journals, papers, and conversations world-wide state no universally accepted definition of leadership exists. There are leadership quotes, guides, training, and billions of records from 720 A.D. to today. There are many forms of leadership, from self, team, or many groups at once, performed by individuals, organizations, teams, companies, and countries. It can be revealed thousands of years after it is performed and forgotten within seconds after being recognized. Something this dynamic must have a foundational definition that works within all use cases and scenarios. Below is this author's attempt to discover this foundational definition. Please join this author and publisher within the social media sphere to expand, explore, confirm, or break this down to a final and acceptable universal definition of leadership.

Leadership is the act of influencing (with actions, sounds, or data), **resulting in a difference,** (in thought, perception, or direction) **causing a change** (in action, results, or being) **measured by movement** (thoughts, ideas, action, and other performance indicators).

TABLE OF CONTENTS

Chapter One

———— ✄ ————

KEY

EVERY THURSDAY NIGHT, thousands of United States Marines gather in groups and clean. They clean everything from living spaces, workspaces, uniforms, and weapons. The lucky Marines even clean the rocks along the walking path or scrape and paint everything from pipes to walls. Group cleaning activities are some of the few universal tasks in every branch of the United States military. The Marine Corps calls its weekly event Field Day. The inspection is the next morning. The cleaning process is typically group-based, labor-intensive, and detail-oriented. Field Days were my first regular exposure to leadership and group dynamics.

Anyone who has spent time working with a large group of diverse people knows, from firsthand experience, how a few people can look busy and accomplish nothing. In contrast, others perform most of the work. In a few years, I would learn this was a living example of the Pareto principle or the 80/20 rule. This rule tells us approximately 80 percent of results are derived from 20 percent of people or effort. At the time, I was impressed by how much effort people would put into doing nothing but trying to look busy. It did not take long to identify the people in our group who were interested in getting the task done as fast as possible, those who were just there and would help if pointed in the right direction, and those who found a way to disappear. It became easy to leverage those who wanted to work and mitigate or ignore those trying not to work.

We lived in Building 1620 at the Marine Air Combat Center. This was an exceedingly long, one-story concrete barracks built during World War Two. One long, open living space is split by two sizeable communal showers, two rows of toilets, and sinks. Each side of the building held sixty Marines in an open bay and one enlisted junior leader in a partitioned room at the far end. It was a Thursday night and time for one of the most unpopular traditions in the Marine Corps, Field Day. Field Day is a weekly event focusing on the entire unit cleaning its rooms. It is common when you are not in the field and a single Marine or living in the unit's communal living quarters. Clean living quarters establish a basic level of expectation, discipline, and disease- and germ-free environment; failing a Friday morning inspection can make for a miserable weekend and may even impact your ability to get promoted over time.

The two junior leaders running the building picked the Marines they trusted to manage the many required Field Day tasks—the young Marines of Building 1620 completed that week's Field Day with no issues. Everyone was heading to San Diego or farther south that weekend, so by all the measurements available in 1986, the Marines of Building 1620 in Twentynine Palms, California, had a successful Field Day.

That Field Day was a non-event outside of the few of us. Nothing special happened, but this was the beginning of my leadership journey in my first career. I was "volunteered" to lead a group of Marines. I became the junior leader's regular volunteer to run a project. Many leaders pick the same few people they trust to help them lead special projects or manage the complexity of today's environment. They are the "go-to people." Picking one or very few numbers of people to lean on as a leader was a learned behavior and made success easy.

It took over a year; I was fully trained as an electronic technician, military occupational specialty 5963, and working on the AN/TYQ-2 Tactical Air Operations Central System. A fully deployable air defense/air traffic control radar system providing positive radar and air control services for military aircraft during combat, tactical training, and routine flight operations. It coordinated air assets with ground-based missiles and Marine, Navy, Air Force, and multinational air forces. It was in service from 1964 until after Desert Storm in the early 1990s. One of the most modern features of the system was the Univac CP 808 computer, which still worked terrific in 1991.

My first permanent duty station was the school, so I had yet to have the opportunity to spend time in the field as a young Marine. The few years I spent in the headquarters element of the Marine Corps Communications and Electronics School influenced my leadership style for decades. I had the opportunity to have the ten-thousand-volt cathode ray tube power supply that ran the radar displays reach out and "touch" me more than once. We saw the *Challenger* shuttle disaster live on TV and had a few earthquakes; I taught my first lab and learned firsthand how dangerous some daily activities can be.

The school was built on the side of the hill within a fenced compound. Between the "upper" system and the "lower" system were four large A/C converters with a direct line to the base power plant. These converted the standard sixty-cycle AC power to the three-phase 400-cycle power required by our systems. One early Saturday morning, another Marine and I needed to set the lower system up for that weekend's operator training class. He was a mid-level leader, E-5, or sergeant. Unfortunately, his rank was not based on experience or knowledge but on his contract, which guaranteed that rank after a few short years.

With the slam of three large breakers, the morning quiet was overtaken by the hum of two of the four large AC converters. I was heading into the building that holds the lower system to turn everything on and make sure it worked and was ready for the training class. The large AC converters are loud enough to be heard a few miles away. Since they are less than a few dozen meters across the parking lot, they provide a continual and predictable background white noise within the building.

We had about an hour to set everything up. The systems were enclosed in heavy boxes with a door on the side—something similar to a standard forty-foot truck container. We were using only twelve of the fifteen operator stations. The lower system was drawing just under 200 kW of 115/205 VAC, 400 cycle power via our single J-2573 power distribution box from the two converters. I was ready to leave the last system box and was confident that everything was prepared for the class.

Just then, the entire system moved a few inches with a loud explosion; it got eerily quiet, and the building was full of black smoke. I could not immediately find the young sergeant. However, it was painfully clear that he tried to take a cable off the distribution box and did not make sure the breaker for that cable was in the off position. He shorted all three phases of power from both converters to the ground. His actions tripped off the two large converters in the parking lot and the base power plant and left a large power cable melted on the concrete. No one had any power; we were missing a person, there was maybe a fire, no working fire alarm, and no one else was in the building yet. I had a big problem to solve, and details matter.

Not a year later, I was tasked with tracking the maintenance equipment. Everyone had additional duties, and it was my turn to oversee the test equipment cage with a considerable number of test equipment and tools. I had already learned my leadership rule number one: find key people to leverage in solving problems. Lesson two: pay attention to training and details; lives may depend on it. I was learning my leadership lesson three, which is that you need to understand the processes in detail and leverage them.

After spending several days finding all the test equipment, I had to inventory all the toolboxes and sign for everything. It did not take long for me to realize we had multiple generations of the same test equipment, and we needed and used less than half of the equipment on hand. I worked with our supply point of contact and, with her help, used a couple of specific supply-type processes, reduced the amount of equipment by a significant amount, and "saved" a lot of money. In the middle of the effort to reduce our excess test equipment, a very expensive and large logic analyzer came up missing from my weekly inventory. I had to report it missing, and a criminal investigation started.

My career was not looking good at this point. I was interviewed by Agent Smith and Agent Smith (yes, they gave me those names) from the Naval Criminal Investigative Service (NCIS) several times. It became apparent that I was suspect number one and must have it. At one point, they showed up at my house while I was at work and ransacked it, looking for the missing equipment. Soon after, a senior enlisted person in the maintenance shop scheduled another person and me to show up on a random Saturday morning to "fix the air-conditioning ducts." I was sure this was more evidence my career was not gaining steam.

Just one hour into the Saturday morning exercise, a senior shift leader staff sergeant (E-7) walked into the same building with the missing test equipment, intending to hide it. I never saw him again after that day, but the base newspaper did print the results of his legal issues later that year. I learned firsthand the importance of being open and honest as a leader. It was time for me to re-enlist and move on to the fleet Marine Corps. I was moving on to Okinawa, Japan.

I was promoted to corporal (E-4). When I arrived at my new command, I was notified that I was awarded a Navy Achievement Medal for my time at the school. Every officer and most senior enlisted wanted to know how that happened because they had never heard of it. I survived that introduction to every officer and senior enlisted in my new unit within the first week. After my inquisition, I almost felt terrible for a couple of the other new officers and enlisted Marines who fell for the challenge of cutting a coin in half with an axe while blindfolded.

I soon developed a solid routine, finding a couple of Marines to leverage as my go-to people and solving the day's problems. I could solve many backlog maintenance items because of the knowledge I gained at the school. I was technically very good at my job but new to this Marine field routine. That was a challenging year for many reasons. I found out my mother was ill, but the hardest time at that point was finding one of the Marines on my team after he committed suicide on watch one night. It did not make sense to me then. We had a high-performing team, and it took years to understand how the environment negatively influenced some people.

Many years later, during Operation Desert Shield, I deployed on the USS *Spartanburg County* as a member of the aviation command and control element of Marine Aircraft Group 40, 4th Marine Expeditionary Brigade. When we transited the Suez Canal, I was finally promoted to sergeant, a mid-level leader. By then, I had mastered identifying key people to help solve my problems. I used this tactic successfully aboard the ship and as part of a small group needing to unload our equipment from the *MV 2nd Lt. John P. Bobo* cargo ship. The Coast Guard Reserve unit was not moving cargo. The reserve unit from my hometown was unhappy with the port's conditions. So, a small group of us learned how to unload the ship and did it in record time. At least that is what the award stated since I do not remember much other than laughing at the guys learning how to operate the crane, the strange feeling of watching a ballistic missile fly by, and the sound a Patriot antiaircraft system makes right next to you, not sleeping for a long time, and borrowing a few trucks. I remember something about the U.S. Army yelling gas a lot, and we ignored it—the British soldiers who passed through and how little I understood what they said.

The finding go-to people leadership tactic worked well when providing maintenance and perimeter security for our forward air controllers of Task Force Ripper in Desert Storm. It worked while transiting minefields, clearing, and setting up operations at the Ahmad al-Jaber Airbase during Desert Storm. Poor leaders were quickly identified and marginalized. All successful leaders and I employed the tactic of having "go-to" people during many stressful activities, environments, and actions in this combat environment. I even had the pleasure of "finding" explosives a couple of times that should have made a significant difference in my life. It was clear to me I used a few of my nine lives. But this idea of leadership was getting easier as time passed.

One of the more unique leadership challenges involved my driver getting scared. I was the passenger in a standard five-ton truck in the middle of a convoy moving from Saudi Arabia to Kuwait that involved passing through what was marked as blue breach two of an extensive minefield. The driver stopped in the middle of the minefield, splitting our convoy in half. After a few choice words of encouragement, it was clear that he did not want to be there and was ready to find a new position. My initial reaction was to get out, go to his door, and help him find his new role in this convoy. I opened my door and saw a large green anti-tank mine and a small, lighter shade of green antipersonnel mine in the sand right under the stepdown. My first thoughts were that mine looked brand-new, and I was not leaving that door at that point. I needed an alternative solution to help get our truck and the second half of the convoy moving. Leadership required an alternative solution from my initial reaction.

My three-step leadership lessons worked. I survived. I have many memories from that experience and wonder "how" over many of them. Like everyone else, I have regrets and lessons learned that I will never forget, some large and some small. I left the combat zone with only a few stitches on my left hand, my personal life in shambles; however, no one died. At least not until we got home.

REFLECTIONS ONE

1. What are the three leadership rules in this text?
    Do you agree with them?

2. There are several leadership "challenges" with no resolution.
    What is your resolution to these challenges? Have you seen or had
    a challenge with a similar solution?

3. Have you been in a situation where the initial reaction or option
    you wanted to employ to solve a problem was unavailable? How
    long did it take to get to the next option, and did it work?

4. Is there an overarching leadership theme that stands out in this
    text?

5. Can you identify a leadership definition or theory within this text?

Chapter Two

———— ❧ ————

LEADING AND RELATIONSHIPS

SOMETIMES, LEADERSHIP FAILURE is challenging to identify because it may manifest itself subtly or not be visible to the leader. The long-term negative impacts of a leader may never be known or measurable by an organization. My firsthand experience working within what seemed a positive and high-performing team based on every measurement used at the time still created an environment that did not build up all of the staff in a positive and life-giving way. We wanted to win and thought we were winning in every way, making great Marines and leaders. Every measurement but one indicated we were on the correct path to success. No one looked at that measurement, even when it was right in front of us.

Understanding the implications of today's decisions may never be known or take years to recognize. Failure can be found in the mistakes made by your team that should be easy to see and prevent. Alternatively, leaders can fail dramatically with one insignificant action or slowly follow the wrong path over time. Failure may be the loss of growth and opportunities for some followers or so drastic that it could lead to loss of life. The leader and the relationship with the followers can make the difference between failure and success; sometimes, success is not just the task at hand but the long-term impact your actions leave on those around you. The more I learned and practiced leadership, the more I understood my simple few steps to leadership were not always the answer.

For many years, my understanding of good leadership started with the ability to identify key people to help manage the day's problems. When I initiated my doctoral journey in strategic leadership, I was an acting executive in a large and well-known federal agency. Experience validated the idea that I needed to find and leverage the high performers on every new journey. I would lean on them until I could lead with as little help from them as possible. It worked from my early three- and five-person teams to places where a decision impacted more than a thousand employees. I was doing it wrong for years. Are you?

Leadership is dynamic and does not require a second individual, specific intent, action, or desired results. It is not based on a specific title, space in an organizational chart, defined time frame, or design. Even in the strictest top-down environments, others will lead something at some point. One individual or entity cannot lead everyone all the time. Leadership requires a leader and a follower, and a good leader is also the follower of themselves.

PRIMUS INTER PARES – FIRST AMONG EQUALS

At the beginning of any leadership journey, every person has a set of tools and possible paths. A leader's toolset could be as simple as their dominant physical size and strength or as complex as an in-depth understanding and application of every leadership theory and practice known. Their paths are determined by their internal bias, desires, needs, and influences of those around them. People will lean on the lessons from others, experience, and internal bias unless trained and practiced to the point of embedded muscle memory of a specific leadership style or path.

Over time, everyone's tools will change and grow based on knowledge, natural talents, and experience. Most leaders desire to succeed; however, success is determined by those who measure the change caused by a leader's actions and the influences they have on others. Not every observer of a change, including the leader themselves, will perceive the difference the same and may not even characterize it as equally good or bad between any given set of observers. This is why you have different opinions on the success of the same leader within various groups. Everyone can identify an event where one group was excited by the observed change while others reacted negatively. Sports, award winners, anyone?

That is the point. Do you not believe that people can see things differently from each other or not recognize what is happening at any point in time? In his research, videos, and books, Professor Daniel Simons uses the phrase *inattentional blindness*. It is the fantastic ability of the human brain not to see or recognize anything that is not expected. If this concept is new to you, please take a moment and check your favorite Internet search engine for videos on the invisible gorilla or the monkey business illusion. Simons has a fantastic set of books and videos that explain his research. Knowing his results is essential since leaders are human and will always miss the unexpected things around them. This is why a group of firsthand witnesses of an event can have a different version of an event. They perceive based on their bias and expectations and not all of the actions in front of them.

RESULTS

Can you see the full results of your actions as a leader? Many leaders may only hear or recognize one version or set of reactions to a change. They may only look for one result or their desired outcome. This recognized response, along with internal biases and perceptions, informs a leader if they are successful. A leader achieving performance metrics may seem successful to everyone except those negatively influenced by the actions taken to get to that metric. As a result, many observers will have a different perception of the leaders' level of success. Self-evaluation and understanding of one's skills and capabilities are difficult to understand fully, and actions may have unintended consequences that the leader may never know. Leadership is more than having talents and abilities and meeting desired short-term goals.

Having all the knowledge and making the correct decisions is one of many factors involving success or failure. An individual leader may get everything right and still fail. Failure may be caused by other people's work or influences outside their knowledge or control. The longer anyone is in a leadership position, the more opportunities they will have to see or experience someone, intentionally or not, causing someone else to fail or look like a failure for the benefit of others. On one occasion, I had an employee go to my boss and convince him that he could do my job at a lower cost with the same results. I was let go. It was a great learning experience for everyone involved. Six months later, I was able to fix everything that was done wrong by that former employee at a new company and a higher salary and cost to my former employer than if I stayed. I grew a lot as a leader and learned how to interact with executives/owners at that new company. It was the right move for me at the right time. Can you be an effective leader by making others look bad?

I also know people in leadership positions who have learned to survive by never putting anything in writing to avoid anyone accidentally or purposely using that against them in the future out of the text's original intent or context. I know people who made all their measurements of success for decades with that and similar approaches to leading. Do you believe that approach is a component of an excellent leadership system?

Occasionally, a leader will make a mistake, and they may never forget those impacted by their decision. I will never forget dozens of events and would do differently if I had the opportunity. Regret is part of the growing and learning process. There is something about leadership that changes the perspective of everything, especially when leadership failure has real-world consequences. For years, we have heard many definitions of leadership. None of those I heard fit outside the concept or environment they are developed to explore or define. A description of leadership involving a group or others did not apply to my self-leadership needs. There is an excellent chance that a great leadership quote from General Patton would not expedite getting the truck driver mentally stuck in a minefield to move that vehicle.

DEFINITION

Despite thousands of years of leadership practice, research, studies, and training, people have yet to develop a widely accepted universal understanding of leadership and how to achieve it.

A version of that statement is in many leadership books, papers, and studies. A quick Internet search of the term leadership will result in more than six billion results. Some individuals and organizations claim a definition, set of steps, or approach to leadership they used, developed, or saw used in a specific instance is the universal definition or approach to leadership. Just do these number of things or that order of task, and you're a leader. Right? I spent most of my leadership career following three basic principles, which worked until it didn't. Do they all work until they do not? Is leadership so straightforward that these simple steps should always work? Yes, if you are only looking for the predicted results. Ignore the monkey in the room. It is all good.

Leadership started in the modern era with traits or skills and has evolved into many scientific-based studies, theories, and applications. The early leaders were the biggest/strongest people in the room or the people who knew how to manipulate those large humans into doing what they desired. Earlier ideas of leadership were based on the relationship between people and the ability to make them move into a desired action. This led to the understanding leadership's most critical components are people and their interrelationships. How does one person interact with another or a group of others to make them do the leader's will? Was the leader manipulating a situation for a desired result, and did it meet a need? The answer to that question is based on your definition of leadership and its desired results.

Like the many concepts of love, leadership requires context for meaning. Any conversation about leaders or leadership must include a foundational definition to baseline and measure success. How can you win without an accepted, universally defined end or goal? A good foundation should be something other than situational, character, or knowledge-specific. There is an old saying that everyone has seen or knows a leader. They are in many different situations, have many different characteristics, and are found everywhere. What is at their core that makes them a leader? Is there a foundation or anything common between self-leadership, business leadership, and individual leaders? A universal definition or foundational framework should fit within that general recognition.

Pick a global or local leader and describe why they are a leader. You will find they impacted someone, themselves, something, or made a difference. Can an organization be a leader? Market leaders like Apple define and are significant influences within a specific market. Organizations like Google, Amazon, and YouTube provide market leadership and form symbiotic relationships with others. Many people have deep-rooted relationships with corporate or national brands and are influenced by them. I have a preferred beverage, and my experience of an event may be different based on the availability of that brand. How my favorite brand interacts with my emotions and perceptions is the same as not recognizing the monkey on a stage. It is my perception based on what I am focusing on at that time.

From the traditional United States perspective, famous individual leaders like Andrew Carnegie, J.P. Morgan, John D. Rockefeller, Henry Ford, and Cornelius Vanderbilt built world-renowned industries that impact the lives of hundreds of millions of people. By all accounts, they are some of the great titans of the American industrial revolution. They created corporations that lead the world, good or bad. They led.

When I was young, we learned how to help others by supporting the work of Saint Teresa of Calcutta. She was a global leader. Many people raised money regularly for her Missionaries of Charity to support her global efforts. It did not take much for her to improve the lives of others. Mother Teresa's work involved more than just meeting basic needs. She provided a simple understanding that everyone had value. Leading others to learn self-worth allowed those individuals to move forward. She was a leader just like the American Industrial Revolution's great titans. Did they all have the same character? Mannerisms? Leadership tactics? Whom do you identify as a leader you recognize now? What did they do? How do they compare? Can you find the common thread?

All these great leaders created a difference, which caused a change in others. You can only lead by making a difference or changing something or someone. This includes leading yourself. Ultimately, every leader has one specific characteristic in their description related to change. They made something different. This common denominator leads to the idea that leadership creates action for change. Leaders are successful facilitators of change. Movement clarifies the direction of the change and the means to measure leadership (action). The one thing that enables stability and allows you to control or manage everything is movement. The ability to continue to move, not fazed by the events around you, enables success. Movement exemplifies leadership, and leaders are always moving forward. Leadership happens when you move.

CAN YOU LEARN LEADERSHIP?

What if we went back to when a trait defined a leader? Many of us would have no chance of being in a leadership role. I, for one, would have never made it into any leadership position. Not many people who met Saint Teresa of Calcutta would say she had many traditional leadership traits. She was not a leader because she was physically dominant over her faithful followers. The good news for most of us is that leadership is teachable. The modern era has many ways, means, and types of leadership training. Go to your favorite Internet search engine and look for learning leadership. You will find more than eight million references.

Leadership requires a knowledge-based situational approach to understanding the environment and the causes of change.

Knowledge-based? You must understand what it takes to go from point A to point B before making the trip or at least have a reasonably thought-out plan or idea. Situational? There is a reason there are over eight million answers to leadership. Leadership takes an approach based on what you have to work with. If time and resources were not a consideration, you could have detailed research and a well-thought-out and rehearsed plan. Since nothing we have is unlimited, you have to make the best decision as soon as you can. Experience will tell you the faster a decision is made, the better leader you will be. Based on a reported Patton quote, I learned early in the military that a good plan violently executed now is better than a perfect plan executed next week. That works every time until you learn the best decision is to do nothing until the time is right. Sometimes, the best plan is to wait to move. You always want to avoid getting in the way of someone else solving your problems, especially if they are the problem.

Movement is recognized and measured using change. Change is the difference measured from one point in time to another.

Once you learn how to influence change, you can learn how to affect and direct change. The military has taught concepts to support this idea of change for over a decade. For example, the average United States Marine did not learn leadership from a book but moved through a defined process. This process is built on traditions and knowledge framed with rules, regulations, and acceptable behaviors. There was never a list of steps. Leadership was making a difference, being better, and striving for that unattainable greatness made by the legendary Marines of the past by learning the influences and changes they made on the institution. Leadership in the Marine Corps is handed down from one generation to the next. In his 1922 letter to his leaders, Lieutenant General John Archer Lejeune exemplified Marine leadership:

> All discreditable occurrences are usually due to the failure of (leaders) to perform their duties properly. Harmonious cooperation and teamwork, with an intelligent and energetic performance of duty, are essential to success. These attributes can be attained by cultivating in your characters the qualities of loyalty, unselfishness, devotion to duty, and the highest sense of honor.

These are characteristics of a good relationship. Putting followers first and leading by example are still foundational components of leadership in the Corps. Putting people first requires action that has a positive influence on the followers. A good Marine is a leader and is always taught to keep moving forward and lead the way.

Much of the leadership training I have seen or taken uses contemporary knowledge of leadership styles and change management theories to create the methodologies or steps needed to facilitate a greater chance of success. Corporate-type management training will typically lean on leadership theories to justify the actions they desire to focus on within a given situation or environment. It reminds me of the person selling a solution without clearly understanding the problem because their answer has a good argument and is ready now. They don't know your issues, but if you buy the idea, book, class, and steps, you will conquer them. Entire industries developed around championing different leadership theories or steps in a training environment. The average Marine in the early 1900s would not have heard of or taken these training classes. However, they still successfully navigated the leadership challenges of the day. They did so by focusing on the Marines in their command and actions that facilitated movement.

Leaders with thousands of followers around the globe or a team of one should recognize that those followers are theirs, not in ownership but in responsibility. They must ensure the followers have the resources and tools to accomplish remarkable things, even if they are their only follower. If you are not leading yourself, then who is? In the Marine Corps example, leaders take ownership of their followers and actions. They practice leadership in the Marine Corps way. They instruct young men and women without specific characteristics, skills, or traits to lead. They have proven that you can teach and learn leadership.

INDIVIDUALS

Humans and every situation are unique. Most modern leadership training and theories treat all followers the same. They expect an individual or group who follows a leader to respond the same to the leader's actions. If you tell a group to go right and they are well-trained, they will all turn right, correct? Did they all turn to point to the same thing? Did they turn until the leader left the room? It will not take long for a leader or other followers to find people who are not entirely on board with their group's direction. Some may participate in the group's activities but never put in all the energy or effort they can. This is often found when a group changes directions with a new leader. Followers could be placating any organizational change or direction until they can return to the old way or change how they want the action done. A follower may do what it takes to get through the day without thinking about anything but going home. Some may be passively or actively going against the leader's direction. Indeed, humans are unique, and nothing a leader can do will change that fact.

The idea that people are vastly unique in many ways—including how they communicate, their biases, and their reactions or responses to interactions—seems intuitive. Unfortunately, this is not a common topic or consideration when discussing leaders and leadership. Most leadership theories, approaches, and training do not consider the individual; they focus on the group of followers as a single organization. There is this idea that a single response or tasking will work the same for everyone in the group. A sizable portion of modern leadership studies stayed with this simple approach toward leadership. They viewed the followers as a single entity with an average understanding and response, requiring only a single approach to achieve the desired outcome with all the individual followers. There is this idea that everyone who follows a specific leader will see and respond to that leader as everyone else in the group does.

For example, the Marines exemplified this concept by proclaiming that everyone who earned their uniform was the single race of Marines with the skin color green. They were one single entity and family for life. There was an expected and similar response from everyone. A Marine in California should react the same way to a primary command as a Marine in a foreign country. They are all trained and continue training as basic riflemen, from those working in the offices to the mechanics, pilots, and cooks. Everyone is a front-line rifleman and a leader. It was God, Corps, country, family, and everything else down the line of importance. This idea that everyone responds the same to a similar stimulus has permeated many cultures and leadership approaches. Those who respond differently are typically not seen in a positive light compared to those who stay in line with the organizational norms. This type of diversity is rarely expected.

Dyad

Organizational complexity and types of work required in the post-industrial age forced many public and private organizations to progress from unskilled labor to a highly skilled workforce. Near the end of the last century, an alternative approach from the standard centralized or authoritative-type leadership model was needed to help understand leadership at the individual follower level and work within this new environment. The world was no longer looking for someone to work mindlessly based on brute force alone.

Before the 1960s, in Western countries, the accepted leadership approaches assumed that all the followers had a singular perspective and received a leader's direction the same. Think of the construction foreman telling a group of shift workers they needed to perform a specific task. The expectation was they performed the task or were no longer part of the team. There was no care or need to concern themselves with the individual perceptions of their followers. As a result, the leader would always behave the same to all the followers. Leaders treated everyone the same, and everyone's response seemed similar, a leadership behavior was typically passed down from one leader to another. This leadership characteristic is based on studies and training before the 1920s. The focus was on the leaders' ability to make a group of people solve a problem. That problem could have been building a widget or winning a war. It was about the group; only the leader was seen as an individual.

Leaders need to understand more about the individual for success in the modern era. Studying human behaviors and group dynamics proved that people were biased toward each other and groups. A new theory was needed to learn how everyone in a group responds to an influence. We needed to do more than have that understanding based on an internal bias that a group always acts a specific way. Entire cultures are built with a similar response concept in mind. Think of societies with a caste-based structure where you were born and stayed in your citizens' class, and it was and will always be that way. It takes a significant amount of understanding of how individuals interact in groups. Leaders did not have the time and energy required to change a culture when there was little understanding of how the culture is formed or maintained at the individual level. How can the leader influence an individual over the focus of running a large team or organization?

The idea that success is influenced by how you perceive the differences in others is relatively new. A leader's bias will influence how they direct and perceive the individual's actions in a group. There is a need to identify, study, and leverage these interactions at the individual level. A successful leader within an increasingly complex environment needs a way to understand, as many as possible, the impacts of actions that influence organizational success. Starting in the 1970s, educators approached this problem using the leader-member exchange (LMX) theory. It helped to understand the influences a leader has at the individual level. The academic world finally correlated the interactions between individuals and how they influenced success. This theory facilitated scientific studies on how leaders and followers perceived and interacted with each other. It helped identify the stages of group formation and interactions between individuals with them.

The theory needed a means to name how people interacted with each other. The early LMX studies identified the unique exchange between individuals within any group as a dyadic relationship. The concept of a dyadic relationship can be confusing when you start working with it. In the basic form, a dyad describes the interaction between two things. In our case, we are looking at a relationship between people. It is human nature that we form relationships and interact with others.

A German sociologist and philosopher named Georg Simmel started using the term dyadic when referring to the interactions between two people. He used this in his study of group formation and the dynamic interactions the groups have on the participants with the groups and others nearby. He needed a term that covered the interaction between the smallest group possible, two. Early in the new leadership theory development, academia focused on the interactions between an individual leader and follower within their dyadic relationship, and studied the exchange between the single leader and member. As a result, our dyadic relationship describes the complex interactions between individual humans involving bias, communications, and influences causing actions.

The more you dive into this concept, the more complicated it gets. However, for our purposes, it is simply a way to describe relationships without knowing their details. Reading this text creates a simple dyadic relationship between the author and the reader based on exchanging ideas, perceptions, reactions, and efforts on these ideas. Sometimes, we need a way to communicate a concept in its simplest form. Using the term dyad is a straightforward way to identify the relationship without understanding the complexities and influences that make up the interactions. A dyad includes direct and indirect communications forming actions and reactions between leaders and followers.

Many LMX studies focused on the relationships, environment, and other factors influencing followers' actions. These studies showed that the interaction between the leader and the followers in a group setting could be the same, radically different, or somewhere between the two. Human psychology and biology, which cover why humans connect or form a connection, are highly complex and are still being discovered in many ways. Those with similar interactions or reactions to an event tend to form groups. Sometimes, these groups involve the leader or members of other groups the leader does not influence. This is primarily based on their commonality compared to each other but can result from any internal or external affinity or influence.

For example, a leader with a group of six may have two people who align well with the leader and form a natural group with that person. Those two could be the ones the leader calls on to get things done or have another common affinity or linkage that binds them. The rest of the team may not perceive the leader badly. However, they are likely not involved in special projects or "high-priority" tasks. We must remember that individuals of any group are influenced and perceived by others based on their social groups, shared identity, or affinity. Two people in the group can have a similar ancestry or other external factors that draw them to form a small group. You can see the formation of groups around sporting events or other competitions.

As you grow the team size, you increase the chance of the members forming different groups separate from the leader's group. Many of these smaller groups will have informal leaders or significant influencers over the groups' membership. Many times, these informal leaders have considerably more influence than the formal group leaders themselves. Studies have shown that small groups can influence their members and other groups around them, and they can develop their characteristics and influence.

When researchers started to view followers' responses to a leader as individuals and small groups, they recognized that not all followers saw the leader the same way or reacted the same. Surprisingly, different people respond differently to the same stimulus. There was this need to identify and quantify small group or individual interactions. These relationships within a group can be very complex. Some of the smaller groups may be temporary. They may be based on relationships involving calendar- or event-based affinity. Think of playoffs in any significant sports league, religious holiday, or connection from natural disasters. All the people engaged in these events will have a different experience than those who are not involved. Those experiences naturally draw each person closer to the others, even if it is just for the duration of the event.

We all understand that not everyone likes the same things and has the same desires or goals; however, most leaders do not apply that knowledge to their organization. Many leaders do not perform based on the understanding that people have views, perspectives, likes, and desires different from their own. They need to recognize that some factions in their organization may follow their leadership desires and others may not, even if they share the same goals and objectives. The larger the organization grows, the less chance there is a single focus on direction, goals, and objectives.

Someone or a group of people no longer following a leader's direction may not be evident by their daily actions. They may quietly placate any organizational change or direction until they can go back to the old way or their way. They may do what it takes to get through the day without thinking about anything but going home. Some may be passively or actively going against the leader's direction when possible. This group lost its total value to the organization once it strayed away from fully accepting and moving in the direction of its leadership. There is a great chance these are from the group of people a leader does not identify as their go-to problem solvers.

Early in my leadership career, I did not know how a leader's actions segmented our teams. I have since learned from concepts from the minimal group paradigm, social identity theory, and other complex leadership theories that identified how destructive a segmented group can be for the entire team. Are leaders unknowingly sabotaging their organizations? Are the perceived top performers negatively impacting your organization? How do you identify the problem, solve it, and keep your organization moving forward?

Studies within the LMX leadership theory proved that focusing on just a few key people in an organization failed the rest of the team members and reduced the organization's overall effectiveness. In contrast, another leadership theory provided viable solutions. Over time, it became clear that positive individual relationships and interactions are essential for organizational success.

GROUPS

Groups are made up of people who are all different in perceptions, interactions, and reactions. They typically comprise followers and a single or small group of leaders. Followers in a group will have positive, neutral, or adverse reactions to leaders. Not everyone gets along with everyone else, and leaders rarely treat their followers the same. Over time, followers will form into small groups. These small groups usually fit within two categories. They are defined as "in" and "out" groups within an organization. Those followers a leader focuses on or naturally aligns well with are identified as the in-group. The out-group are those individuals the leader does not focus on or align well with.

The idea of this out-group is not new. However, some studies show that followers can freely move between groups as their perceptions and situations change. The more people you have in your in-groups, the more people move with you at your speed and vigor. The followers' long-term success depends on their subgroup.

There are examples of these in- and out-groups all around you. If you are a sports fan, think of any event venue where most fans back one team over another. The in-group typically supports the same team as the majority. You will enjoy the pleasures of being part of the majority and be conditionally accepted in their inner circle. How would you feel about those other fans? You may be cordial and polite, but are they received the same as your team fans? Take sports out of the conversation and split a large group of coffee drinkers into groups based on their go-to coffee shop. A follower can be a dedicated fan of the local movie theater over those who watch TV, play video games, or read nightly. Those with a common interest will connect because they have a greater dyadic relationship than those not part of the same group.

Studies related to social identity theory (SIT) reinforce the idea that individuals will naturally segment themselves and others into multiple categories based on various identities at any given time. These studies tell us that most humans form part of their identity based on the group they are identified as, associate with, or participate in. Social identity theory shows that a group affiliation will influence individuals' behavior based on their attachment to the group. We have all worked in an office where you have the boss's favorite: cliques and clubs. Those are the specific "go-to" people for a leader. Those go-to people are the in-group in an overly simplistic view.

But life is not that simple. Group placement highly depends on the leader, the environment they create, and the other influential factors on a follower. The influences of these environmental factors can change as relationships evolve. Followers will fall into groups they can identify with or fit within their perceived identity. A self-described criminal and gang member will not typically hang around and feel comfortable with or quickly join the local church choir or pro-law enforcement group. But that person may feel comfortable or at home within the local criminal organization.

Neurological studies have shown that the brains of leaders and followers react differently when they engage with individuals from diverse groups. This reaction is also a factor in how groups form. People are wired to work better within a particular group than others. It is how humanity has evolved. A Harvard graduate will treat another Harvard graduate differently than a non-graduate. We are all wired slightly differently from each other and learn bias as groups.

There are many ways and reasons people form subgroups like an in-group. Followers self-categorize themselves based on many factors, from race, age, similar likes, social groups, and many other reasons, with some being rational and some not. Organizational subgroups can form based on team affinity and political affiliation. Many leaders force followers into subgroups by creating team-building activities or management styles that pit one office or small group against others or by providing specific opportunities only to a few followers. Some leaders follow forced ranking theories that result in an annual termination of a known percentage of followers based on arbitrary, short-term performance measurements.

How do you build a fully inclusive in-group in a similar environment? There are countless ways a leader can push and guide people into subgroups. Chaos and turmoil are not suitable for positive group development in a long-term, sustainable way.

Individuals use social categorization to understand their identity, the identity of others in their environment, and the identification of in- and out-group members around them. People consciously and subconsciously categorize other people all the time. Some are self-motivated to engage in behaviors that solidify membership within valued identity groups through interaction with other members. We have evolved to find the groups with whom we can feel safe and identify those who may be a perceived or learned threat. We are social animals and need to be in groups that make us comfortable. This is how you find your social groups. You can only bring people into your group if your actions make them desire other members, group actions, or feel safe. Maslow's hierarchy of needs is a well-studied and accepted human needs theory. Humans will gravitate toward groups that meet their individual needs. Recognizing that an organization's needs are not as important as the means toward a follower's basic needs is essential. Suppose a group or organization cannot meet the basic needs of the followers. In that case, followers will move toward another group they perceive will meet those needs.

Followers typically view the group they associate with as good or better than others. In the context of sports, our team is always the good guy, or we want them to be better than the other team. Your favorite place is the best one in your area for no other reason than it is your personal favorite. The groups you associate with bring you value in one form or another. Leaders should provide an environment that brings that value to all the followers in the organization.

People prefer being around other members of their subgroup because psychological predisposition drives them to help those they perceive are similar. They also expect in-kind reciprocation from those in the same group compared to those outside that individual's group. Followers find group membership comforting based on the perception that group membership brings them more security and increases their chance of success. Evolution made sure all humans feel safer as part of a group.

REALITIES

How can humans have different realities from each other based on the same events or data? The bonds within the in- and out-groups are strong enough to influence the group members' perception of reality. Studies have shown that two separate subgroups can watch the same event and have enough group bias to perceive the events differently. They can have different truths on the same set of facts. We all have seen firsthand how people can view the same event and have two diametrically different views of reality based on group affiliation. This is important in the context of leaders and followers and is a critical component of organizational inefficiencies. As a leader, you should want your entire group to work on the same basic assumptions and reality with which you are working.

This inability to recognize a leader's actions the same way between groups reinforces that group membership will influence how followers perform. This different perception of a leader's effort justifies why group members react differently toward leaders. How can you guarantee an out-group member will follow the desired direction if there is a good chance they may not even be working on the same set of foundational facts that you have as a leader? That alone is a great reason a leader should have as many team members as possible as part of their in-group.

Many members of groups can find self-value from the group separate from the goals and objectives of the leader, causing them to be identified as an out-group. Members of an out-group in an organization are typically not aligned with the goals and objectives of its leaders. This lack of alignment creates inefficiencies and gaps between desired and attainable actions and results from the actual organizational performance. This lack of alignment is why understanding this relationship is essential and hard to identify and measure.

Leadership and its long-term impacts are more complicated than a single measurement or event. However, as a leader, it is easy to think back on how much higher the go-to people were with performance and dedication than the rest of the team. Leveraging in-groups is a typical leadership tactic because these people outperform their peers. Realistically, they outperform their peers because they are part of the in-group and not necessarily more talented, gifted, or self-motivated.

It is easy for leaders to focus their perceived best performers on the most critical task. LMX research found that in-groups produce less employee turnover. Members in these groups receive better performance evaluations. They are promoted more, have a more significant organizational commitment, and receive more desirable work assignments. In-group members have better attitudes, receive more attention and support from the leader, and progress further and faster than their peers. The in-group is created by bias and perceptions. If not recognized and appropriately mitigated, leaders' bias or group affinity will impact all followers' long-term social and economic realities.

Placement into one of the groups is not by any commonly accepted discriminatory characteristics such as education, age, sex, race, or education as one would expect. Social identity theory tells us leaders will naturally gravitate toward individuals based on perceived experiences, affinity, and other salient identities that can have nothing to do with their ability to lead or perform in a leadership role. Many times, a leader does not consciously separate their followers into subgroups.

In-group membership requires trust and does not require any specific leadership characteristic. A leader can find trust based on a connection or perceived shared group membership. This shared group may be as simple as an affinity for the same sport or activity. Social identity theory shows us the followers who share this connection will have a greater perception of the leaders' effectiveness, increasing their likelihood of participating within the leaders' in-groups. A leader's initial categorization of group membership is a good predictor of the performance and ratings of the followers.

Group assignments are related to the observations of perceived performance based on the leader's bias. If the leader perceives the actions as trustworthy and attractive, the follower is seen as a better performer and subconsciously placed in the in-group. The perceived low performance of the out-group is commonly ascribed to a lack of ability and not something a leader can quickly correct. There is a perception that the leaders "trust" the followers of the in-group. This perceived trust, or lack thereof, is crucial in subgroup development as it influences the dyadic relationship.

With a basic understanding of subgroups and long-term impacts, it is not difficult to understand the productivity and positive influences lost by the average leader. All those followers in the out-group lost opportunities to learn, grow, and participate in making a positive difference. Millions of followers around the globe on the same day, all not in sync with the mission at hand that day and every day moving forward. The loss of productivity and growth of individuals impacting the future operations of any organization is not measurable. Performance measurements may recognize the loss of productivity. However, the initial cause may not be known or identified.

The early LMX research indicated that those who are not in the in-group perform at a marginal level compared to the in-group members. Every comparative study shows that out-group members have higher turnover rates and are less interested in the organization's success. Out-group members have less fulfilling professional careers than other group members. This means if you have an in-group in your office or organization, you have an out-group and are not performing to your capacity as an organization, which is a problem.

No individual or team is perfect, but the out-group creates unnecessarily lost efficiencies, opportunities, and failed team members. How many people have lost hope and are not connected to a mission, task, or organization because a leader doesn't recognize they have out-groups? The leader may not move an entire group to one large in-group but can provide an environment to influence a reduction in the number of teams lost in the out-group. There are things a leader can learn to create an environment that allows for completing goals and objectives while focusing on the followers to move toward an in-group. This will improve the people the leaders serve, increase productivity, and help followers grow to their ultimate potential. An inclusive workforce will produce more for the organization, themselves, and the larger societal groups than an exclusive workforce.

So, you have or have seen the go-to people in an organization and can now recognize their impact on the group's overall performance. The recognition of a problem is a significant step in solving it. As leaders, we can move forward with a new understanding of our relationships with our followers. With some practice and knowledge of the influences that affect a dyadic relationship, a leader can create an environment where most organizations work as an in-group.

REFLECTIONS TWO

1. What is a dyad and why is it essential?

2. Followers can form groups among themselves within a larger organization. Can you identify the two main groups?

3. Have you been in a situation where you can now recognize the formation of groups?

4. Does an overarching leadership theme stand out in this text?

5. Can you identify a leadership definition or theory within this text?

Chapter Three

INCLUSIVE

INCLUSIVE LEADERSHIP APPLIES leadership practices and characteristics that bring most of an organization into a single in-group. The practical application of inclusive leadership can fit within any situation. However, there is no single checklist or a simple recipe. Leading requires flexibility within our complex and continually changing environment that a simple list or approach cannot provide. Basic tenets associated with servant leadership create a framework that will work with many leadership styles to facilitate an inclusive organization. It may sound simplistic, but a leader needs more than a process; followers must accept and interact to create an inclusive environment. Inclusive leadership is built on the idea that a leader can positively influence all individuals and group formations. Why not focus on what facilitates an inclusive organization?

An inclusive approach does not replace or ignore any organization's standard goals and objectives. On the contrary, a healthy, inclusive organization needs success and growth for itself and its members. A leader of a coffee venue could have goals and objectives associated with quality, sales, and the environment. Nothing stops that leader from attaining those goals while supporting and meeting the needs of the followers to create an inclusive environment.

Creating an inclusive environment does not negate the need for activities and measurements toward an organization's success within its known marketplace. Creating the framework for an inclusive environment may influence how goals and objectives are obtained but never replace them or their intended need. A leader looking to add an inclusive approach should add goals and objectives to the organization and expand what success looks like, not replace what is already known and planned.

Starting Point

The dyadic relationship between leaders and followers is the foundation for developing organizations' subgroups. Groups cannot form where there is no shared resource or information. The influence within the dyadic relationship leads to some form of connection between the group members. Relationships require regular interpersonal communication. This form of communication does not need a formal structure, but it requires all the parties involved to stay engaged and use all elements of the communication process.

Continual engagement in communication by all parties is essential for successful interactions. It can affect more than two people within an organization and find its form in face-to-face dialogue or other communication techniques. Effective communication is not dependent on the role of the individual. However, it is the primary means of influence over others and their groups. A framework that generates continual engagement will succeed more than a one-off or limited applied event or activity.

Leaders are sometimes identified by perception, not by title or placement within a group. Subgroups may have group leaders or influencers within the larger follower community in an organization. Individuals and their character are the primary factors in how communications are received and the development of group dynamics. The perceived leader is the fundamental influencer on group dynamics and the formation of subgroups.

Success as a leader is more than the quality of the decision made. It is how leadership is exercised and the interactions with the followers in reaching these decisions. Self-discovery and personal growth are critical qualities of successful and inclusive leaders. Many people naturally have good leadership tools and activities that can be enhanced through practice like many other learned or natural tendencies. A successful leader can identify gaps in the basic tenets needed for leadership and find ways to close them. Formal and informal training mentoring and other standard tools are readily available and used by many leaders. Anyone can learn and start practicing inclusive leadership at all levels of an organization.

The follower will move closer to an in-group membership based on the quality of the dyadic relationship with the leader. It takes effort on the part of the leader to improve the dyadic relationship, which will result in a better experience for everyone within the group. It does take two or more for communication and a positive dyadic relationship, but the leader is the single most prominent point of failure in any organization since they directly or indirectly influence everyone else. Research has shown that followers can find fulfillment, maintain motivation, and move toward the in-group based on a positive dyadic relationship with leaders. The dyadic relationship is between people, and a leader needs a good connection to create an inclusive environment.

The individuals in a group will experience the highs, lows, losses, and every emotion a human can experience on their schedule. As a leader, you cannot map out or schedule a specific relationship within a defined time frame. A positive relationship requires the parties involved to understand, value, and support each other. Foundational leadership tenets must survive and improve interpersonal relationships with these situations and emotions.

SINE QUA NON: ESSENTIAL

There are ten principles or tenets associated with successful leaders. These are categorized into the five characteristics of vision, care, learning, communication, and action as an inclusive leadership approach. The idea of Vision includes the tenets of awareness, conceptualization, and foresight. Care is based on stewardship and building a community. Learning is healing and a commitment to growth. Communication is listening and empathy. Action is persuasion. These identified tenets are derived from the 1977 text on leadership by Robert Greenleaf. His groundbreaking concepts are the basis for many studies and approaches toward leadership. Many studies have shown that these tenets positively affect an organization and can solve the leadership problems identified by LMX with in- and out-groups. In the simplest form, these are components of a well-studied leadership theory applied as an operational framework to solve a problem identified by a different leadership theory. They are organized and detailed for this solution and are excluded from the details and training associated with the LMX leadership theory.

These are not exhaustive but the foundational tools a leader uses to build high-performing and focused teams. The continual application of these tenets will change a leader and their followers and, as a whole, provide a representative framework for an inclusive leadership approach. This approach will work in a secular and nonsecular environment while offering a better predictor of high-performing teams than a typical LMX approach or solution. A typical leader-follower environment is too large to have the dedicated one-on-one relationship found in a standard LMX-defined solution. The application of a positive approach to these tenets work any time in the life cycle of a team or group and at any level of an organization.

Leaders are often considered the glue that holds an organization together in good and bad times. Usually, a leader will create a shared vision, task, or common theme to maintain an organization's focus on the task at hand. There are ways to develop a team that can lead to a majority, singular in-group, or a globally inclusive environment with all followers.

Just as with the earlier example of the Marines learning leadership by practical application with examples, the focus on providing a positive application of these tenets can teach leadership, leading any organization toward inclusivity. Creating a vision and implementing actions toward a common goal are interrelated and required for an inclusive environment.

Changing how followers form subgroups requires a leader to focus on developing the people following them. A leader can apply the practical tenets to help followers reach their highest potential in organizational and career success. Studies suggest that implementing these tools positively influences characteristics that indicate global in-group acceptance. These tools are also found in standard management and leadership training and components of many modern leadership theories. There are many informal studies, formal research, training, and educational tools to support the application and improvements in any of these areas. It is all about a leader creating a singularly focused and positive community. The more inclusive the environment a leader creates, the more people participate in an in-group.

These areas of focus are needed to manage the complex task of leadership in any environment. It may take years to fully grasp just one of the tenets, let alone practice to the level of mastery. Some of them will come naturally to a leader. That is what makes us human. We are all different and can naturally perform a single characteristic or tenet over another, but a leader can strive to be the best as their abilities allow and continually improve.

No one is the perfect leader in all situations and phases of life. A practicing leader can apply vision, care, learning, communication, and action to develop personal and professional goals. An organization can use them to measure a leader's effectiveness. One can have continual improvements (movement) gained from the application and measurement against them. They can be applied to many aspects of an organization to foster leadership and create an inclusive culture. None of these in themselves are new ideas. It is about taking commonly accepted leadership traits and applying them to make an inclusive environment.

REFLECTIONS THREE

1. Can you explain the characteristics and tenets of an inclusive leadership approach?

2. Have you seen or used any components of an inclusive leadership approach?

3. Is there a component of the approach that you think is missing?

4. Does an overarching leadership theme stand out in this text?

5. Can you identify a leadership definition or theory within this text?

Chapter Four

———— ✺ ————

VISION

CREATING AN INCLUSIVE environment requires leaders to have a motivationally framed and credible vision. A vision is commonly formulated into an articulated set of future-oriented goals built on values. A good vision is practicable, reasonable, and challenging and transforms a group into something better than it is today. This should be the desired improved state and not just a forecast of projected performance. A clear vision will articulate the future state of your group. A leader's vision should be transformative and focus on the organization's imagination and desire to be more significant than what they do today.

Motivation is necessary to have an obtainable goal that gets people excited. There should be a reason for the followers to be vested in the future of their organization. The shared goal attracts a follower to the organization. It may be strong enough to create an affinity for in-group acceptance for some followers. It shouldn't be a negative or a future that is a distraction as it may push followers into an out-group.

Training on the expected path to the future and not just advocating a vision will help gain the full support and buy-in of the team. There are many ways to develop a vision and vision statement. Books, studies, and consultants can guide you through a process, or you can apply a conceptual framework that will result in a statement or guiding principle. This is not about a one-time statement. In the context of servant leadership, it is about the continual development and growth process we take as leaders and guide our teams through. This is how we define ourselves and those around us.

A vision must fit within acceptable ethics and morality. If the vision is not accepted, it will cause more harm than having no vision. Followers who are ethically and morally opposed to a vision or portion of it will undoubtedly find their way into an out-group, if not outside or against the organization. However, several studies show that success includes an accepted and compelling vision. A leader develops this vision by continually applying strategic foresight, awareness, and conceptualization while applying the art of systematic neglect and intuitive insight. What does this mean at a high level?

Your Changing World

A leadership approach moving toward an ideal future provides more control, improves the organization, and helps facilitate a common identity for the entire organization. An identified and generally accepted long-term perspective can provide that common thread for group cohesion. Long-term planning typically looks five years out and includes a projected number of sales or other measurements of success and budgets. Looking into the future, specifically, strategic foresight looks ten or more years out. This long-term perspective is not preparing for an inflexible forecast of a well-defined future. Foresight provides the understanding needed to make the correct decisions today to set the organization up for the best future. It is a process that offers several possible futures and their impacts on an organization.

Strategic foresight will help identify essential things today and provide a framework for tomorrow's decisions. The process will also allow an organization to view possible futures and validate that the short-term plans fit the desired outcomes and should include the impact on the followers. Strategic foresight is applying a set of tools with an approach that focuses on the leaders' thinking for facilitating engagement to discover possible futures. There are no predefined steps or a small group of simple things to answer questions. Several different tools that are situationally dependent are available for this approach. These tools will allow an organization to frame expectations, opportunities, and threats with mitigating actions.

The idea of foresight is not to identify where today's plans will take your organization. Foresight is an exercise to look at potential future end states based on external pressures and market predictions to ensure your current path is sustainable.

Strategic foresight is based on the early work of Herman Kahn at the RAND corporation's first think factory in the 1960s. Edward Cornish and others then proliferated this strategic foresight concept in the early days of futurist papers, magazines, and then society. Many institutions, universities, and federal agencies tested and refined the futurist ideas and tools used. These early years were in the middle of the Cold War, and many people believed that nuclear war was inevitable. Edward Cornish was obsessed with changing the future and understanding how studying future possibilities might cause world peace. He wanted to find ways to identify a future that included world peace and show it was a possibility. This future would then provide the possible decisions needed to obtain that desired end state. He wanted to find ways to research the future to make a difference.

There is no definitive or single answer to what the future may bring to an organization. Strategic foresight will provide many potential futures to help organizations make informed decisions and strategic plans. Just as Mr. Cornish wanted to find his desired end state, any organization can use the same set of tools to locate the desired end state that includes an inclusive environment. The World Future Society and the text by Edward Cornish (2004), *Futuring: The Exploration of the Future*, provide a great starting point for an in-depth understanding of foresight.

In a leadership framework, conceptualization is like looking toward the future. It can look beyond the regular daily activities but stay within the current time frame and context to identify new perspectives on the same topic in order to understand the significant factors influencing the current organizational state. Knowledge of these factors will foster an environment to expand the organization's perspective on the impacts of decisions today that are not readily recognized.

There are always unintended consequences of every action in a complex environment. Visualizing a different view from your own allows a leader to acknowledge bias and impacts that they may have otherwise missed without this perspective. This effort can take a leader past the focus on the day's short-term goals and see the bigger picture.

Closely related, awareness is understanding some information and how it directly or indirectly impacts a specific target. Awareness is usually more critical to a leader's success than any technical skill or intelligence quotient (IQ). This is why the most intelligent person in the room is not always the most successful. Grasping this big picture allows a leader to perceive multiple perspectives simultaneously. This perspective includes the ability of the leader to understand the impacts of their personality traits, quirks, and default responses to actions that affect those around them. Awareness allows a leader to identify areas that need growth and recognize the impacts of the actions taken.

Specifically, self-aware leaders make better decisions, perform in line with the team, and balance the needs of others and the organizational goals. One of the best ways a leader can grow awareness is by soliciting, accepting, and leveraging feedback. This ability allows a person to view any topic with great inclusivity. A common tactic for this feedback is found in the form of a 360 review that provides self-assessments and external assessments on the same topics from others. If appropriately implemented and accepted for action, this is a valuable tool for leading an inclusive organization.

The purpose of an inclusive leader is to maintain that day-to-day perspective in balance with a larger picture and how they impact others in the group. An inclusive leader accomplishes this task by keeping that everyday mindset in harmony with the larger view and recognizing how their actions affect others.

Every action you take as a leader can impact those who follow you. Leaders can reflect on their actions, consider how they would react, and learn how others may respond to help understand the impacts of those actions. But predicting all the results of an action is not possible. There are too many variables, and many of them are not known. Once a leader has these potential reactions and context, there needs to be a way to leverage them for the organization's good. This is one of those skills that require practice, resulting in experience and external feedback.

Knowledge with no action has limited to no value. Many times, the most critical task a leader can do is decide. Do not let the lack of an apparent picture cause indecisiveness. A lack of decisions is a lack of progress. There is no way to determine all the results and impacts of every decision when humans are involved, but decisions are required for movement.

Systematic Neglect

A vision includes the use of resources, and resources are limited. A critical component of leadership is identifying the task needed to complete an objective. Inclusive leadership does not waste resources, including the efforts of the followers. The art of systematic neglect sounds very harmful and destructive to many people, and in specific contexts, it is not a good approach. The positive leadership version is the culmination of the skills and art of understanding for choosing to neglect the activities, events, or meetings that are not critical. Inclusive leadership is not just about deciding; the inclusive leader will make decisions that do not waste time, effort, and other resources.

Systematic neglect in this context is the understanding and ability to recognize the activity not required for success. This is the business application of the 80/20 rule, also known as the vital few or Pareto principle. The Pareto principle indicates that only a tiny portion holds the most value, about 20 percent of anything. This process is a means to identify those required tasks. The Pareto principle is an accepted and universal understanding of operations and is considered the norm in economics, marketing, sales, quality control, operations, and many other organizational settings.

Systematic neglect is helpful for any situation with a cause-effect relationship. It requires an understanding of the likely future effect of any cause. In the most complex application, this involves identifying the probable future results and identifying the factors that can cause them in order to narrow them toward the most critical few for action.

Suppose a leader understands just the most vital tasks and decisions. In that case, they can keep the team from doing mundane and unnecessary activities. In the simplest form, systematic neglect is learning those activities or norms used by others that are not required for an inclusive and prosperous result. They can be an application of lessons learned.

Intuitive insight is the judgment of a subject of observation when the results are unknown. This insight is not an analytical or step-by-step form of understanding a problem, but a mix of lessons learned, observations, knowledge, and skills resulting in an idea with no definitive reason for how or why. This is typically that internal voice that tells one to do something. The action turns into the correct or best path forward. Intuitive insight allows leaders to make decisions toward a more inclusive environment. Understanding the information at hand, possible solutions, and outcomes can provide a leader with enough information to formulate and maintain a positive vision—one that is inclusive, transformative, and focuses on the organization's imagination with little waste or negative impacts.

Leaders should have an inclusive vision for themselves and their followers. Keeping that vision within the ethical norms of the entire organization will move more followers toward a singular in-group while moving the organization forward. Taking the time and effort to ensure you are protecting the limited resources of the followers will improve the dyadic relationships.

Chapter Five

CARE

MOST LEADERS ASSUME the person who receives care reaps the benefits at the expense of the person providing care. Caring for others benefits the leader and followers when it is a choice and when support is perceived to be effective. Having an inclusive environment requires a leader to care. Caring for others will gain the most productivity from them. You cannot fake genuine concern for others. Caring for your team requires stewardship and community. As a leader, you can provide an environment for a sense of community or destroy a community. You cannot build a community on your own or by declaration. Creating a sense of community in a highly anxious or stressful environment is an obvious and reasonable approach to increasing productivity and inclusiveness. Community is a concept that is hard to define to fit every application. A community is recognizable and inclusive of its members, and inclusive leadership will result in a community.

Community

"Community" has many meanings based on different perspectives, from politics to religion. Some philosophies advocate that communities are groups of few known contributors for a common cause or maintain similar characteristics. A community is an organization with a group identity that instills a sense of belonging and security in this context. It is not a place but a group of people who have a shared allegiance or culture and do not want to let the other members down.

In a community, people will care about and for different people. Personal perceptions are more influential than location and may be perceived negatively if not appropriately managed. A community is fallible. It is made up of people and will never function as a single entity all the time. Group fallibility is one factor that allows subgroup members to move from one group to another. None of the negative traits of a community will negatively impact the overall positive features that having a community will bring to an organization.

Communities have a meaningful sense of purpose, and individual members are more connected to the organizational goal. A leader can build a society where the least skilled task is as important as the most skilled task. This shared community will advance the diversity of thought and overall organizational inclusiveness. An inclusive environment is not a majority rule and does not accept performance at the lowest common denominator. Building an inclusive community is different from traditional business norms. It requires a new way of being for many organizations, and it needs structure. However, it cannot survive an authoritarian leader or micromanaged tasks.

Creating an inclusive environment is still more common than having that positive community for many organizations. Many leaders say they operate in a shared community environment, but unfortunately, most people in the United States believe they are not working within a community.

The leader's action or created environment does not develop a community. Building a community requires leadership involvement, creating gathering spaces or town hall-type events that foster team membership, communicating a vision, and connecting with the team members. The majority of a community must be willing to support each other regardless of roles, be good toward each other, and interact with an acceptance of a set of shared values. A leader must encourage the communications and interactions required to build and maintain the desired shared value.

Helping others pushes an organization to grow closer together as a community. Most times, the community is more about the people around an organization than internal members. It is more about the whole and not just a few. Leaders and followers need to stay involved with others. Doing something as simple as taking one day a year to volunteer as a group, holding food drives, and providing mentorship and internship for the youth living near your groups, alongside standard philanthropy efforts, will instill pride and foster a sense of goodwill. That level of caring is contagious while providing an opportunity for team-building exercises and shared experiences. Allowing the team to determine the charities brings leaders and followers at all levels into an active participant role in the community. Group philanthropy will enable a culture of giving. Shared cultures can provide the catalyst for in-group development.

People look for communities to connect with others in an organization, learn from them, and have a holistic perspective on fitting within the overarching goals and objectives. There needs to be an understanding of need and belonging. People need an opportunity to participate and gain recognition for that participation and development of in-groups. Awareness will ensure that the options are available and used. A feedback loop is required within any community to ensure that goals and values are shared and met. The individual connection within the circle between members and leadership will define people's values and shared meaning. It is still about leaders and followers understanding that they are individuals with their values, needs, and perceptions.

COLLABORATION

Collaboration can be the cause or result of an organization or environmental structure where diverse skills and individuals interact. This is a catalyst that forms a group of people into a community. The interactions between individuals are motivated by self-service or in the organization's best interest. Collaboration requires the focus on the organization and not the individual. This idea that the organization and those around you are more important than your desires and goals is the foundation of the relatively new management stewardship theory, which started in the early 1990s to explain the relationship between ownership and leadership in a corporate environment but has had an expanded application since then.

From a military perspective, this is the concept of fighting for your team alongside them in the foxholes and not some self-guiding principle or national goal. In a less violent application, the behavior places a higher value on the collective than on individuals. Organizations and individuals can see gains with pro-organizational behaviors. This makes sense because every person in a group can succeed if that group succeeds. They are working together for a common cause.

Stewardship is suitable for success as the participating members are pro-organized and reliable. Critical components of organizations that foster stewardship empower team members and maintain an inclusive environment. The long-term understanding of stewardship is taking care of or being responsible for something without ownership. As a leader, you are responsible for your team but do not own or fully control them. A good leader understands they are the team's stewards, cares enough about them, and does not waste the gifts the group members bring toward the whole.

Chapter Six

———— ✦ ————

LEARNING

UNDERSTANDING AND COMMITTING to the advancement of others can show they have value more than what they produce or provide in return. This commitment to the growth of others leads to an environment of learning for all parties involved. In many ways, the ideas of learning and teaching are interchangeable concepts in that those who teach will learn. Leaders who engage in the experiment of learning with followers will learn and improve the dyadic experience with these interactions. Followers learning from or facilitated by leaders share the experience.

Inclusive leaders will do everything to grow followers in all facets of their being. The practical application is funding continuing education and bringing diverse educational opportunities into the organizational environment while fostering a solid mentorship program.

Most organizational training focuses on effective management rather than leadership. However, there is value in focusing on leadership over management training within organizations. The United States Marine Corps established, teaches, and operates with a base set of minimum expectations. These manifests themselves as expected responses to standard orders. A Marine in Ohio will respond similarly to the same order as a Marine in Europe or the Far East. The Marine Corps teaches future leaders to expect and only accept the correct reactions; they teach and perform daily with the same expectations, which is part of their leadership brand. They build leaders who can solve a problem at all levels with little to no direction based on already known expectations and norms. Leaders can establish their followers' brand as leaders by teaching and expecting leadership at every level. An inclusive leader will involve all the followers in the leadership experience at every opportunity.

One of the hardest lessons to learn in leadership training is letting go. An inclusive leadership style requires the leader to provide the environment necessary for the followers to complete their tasks. The key is not the leader completing the task but providing the basic knowledge (training), tools, purpose, key tasks or activities, and a clear goal for the followers to achieve. Then, let them achieve it. The United States Marine Corps accomplishes this by providing everyone with a standardized set of basic knowledge and tools required for a typical general task. Therefore, every Marine is taught basic infantry skills and tactics.

The specific task or set of orders given to followers will always include a big-picture purpose, risk, key tasks, or critical path of known activities (enemy actions, intention, vulnerabilities) and a clear goal. This is commonly known as the commander's intent, and it allows the followers to have all the information required to make decisions along the team's journey and still solve the actual problems.

Leadership training is more than providing the tools to solve a simple task. It requires all the knowledge and skills needed to let your followers meet clear goals and keep everything moving.

Leaders who focus on leadership training are successful because of a focus on leadership and people over well-trained managers. Well-trained managers learn the process of an organization in its current state and how to maintain the current state efficiently. Managing a known or sedentary process and keeping daily activities will not move an organization to something new. Leaders around the globe are continually learning that if they are not progressing forward, they are left behind.

Blockbuster was a famous chain of video rental stores that made a lot of money managing memberships and late fees on video rentals. They had many locations where members could walk in, pick a movie on a VHS cassette format, and rent it for a day or three. The profits were so significant that Blockbuster did not consider transitioning toward a digital online market, thinking they would lose too much money in late fees. The competition was going digital with a business model of mailing to the home from an online catalog or neighborhood vending machine. It did not take long for the new format and business model to overcome the video rental store concept, and Blockbuster slowly went out of business. On the contrary, the mail-to-home-based CD rental provider continually moved forward with the technology and marketplace and successfully transitioned toward a pure digital online business model.

Followers learn and operate how they are trained and expected to perform. Teaching and learning leadership creates the opportunity for an inclusive environment while providing for organizational success. The movement associated with improvements will generate long-term success compared to those organizations that only teach and learn sustainment process management.

Learning an existing process and procedure has short-term value, but it does not foster any long-term improvements or growth needed for leadership. There needs to be a bigger-picture perspective on the topic over most generally accepted process management, training, and education. Inclusive leadership works best when taught, learned, and operated consistently.

PAUCITY

Scarcity is absolute, and there is a gap between limited resources and needs in every environment. This reality requires decisions about how to allocate resources efficiently. The people identified as the target for leadership training are as important as the topic. The target audience for growth can make a substantial impact on an organization.

Most continuing education or corporate-type training typically goes toward those already well-educated. In the world's population, those with a degree are less than 7 percent; however, an organization's percentage of educated members is related to its success. A leader should allocate limited training resources to those in the most need over those already trained. Training the educated does not provide the most value. Evidence shows that leaders who target the most junior followers for training and education see the most value from that effort. There are a lot of positive results from these focused approaches. It makes sense that those with the lowest amount of training will gain the most out of some training since they have the most significant knowledge gap on the topic at hand.

Offering training is not a guarantee for success. Many organizations attribute success to training on a specific topic or teaching methodology but cannot measure this for validity. Unfortunately, correlation is typically the determining factor in identifying the actual cause of the positive impacts. There is this assumption that if you completed training and then had success, the training must be the cause of the success. It is challenging to determine that training material was the exact cause of the improvements because too many variables are associated with group leadership.

Some studies do make a direct correlation between training activities and progress. The success may be a byproduct of team interactions during training, a diversionary tactic from the daily norms, or coincidental. Complexities from the environment, education, bias, nationalities, and other factors impact how activities focusing on growth will affect any individual or group.

There is considerable evidence that there is some value in training the least educated group first. This approach allows an organization to strive for a minimum baseline of education and training to create a common reference point. Baseline or standard training is a catalyst for group cohesion and development. The least trained first is the best approach toward targeted training. The value may be with the motivation and perception provided to a follower by just having the opportunity to improve and not the improvement activity. Improvement is more than just training. It helps solve the impediments to a successful organization, shows that employees have value, and moves the trained individuals forward in their lives and careers.

HEALING

Every group will have some level of flaws that impact success. The idea of healing is not found in most literature or training on leadership. Healing in leadership is so foreign and confusing to many people that it is separate from any significant assessment of leaders or leadership performance.

When followers' dreams, hopes, cares, goals, and objectives are not realized as expected, their dyadic relationship will falter. They become broken and damaged and need healing, impacting their ability to interact with others. Followers must overcome broken and damaged dyadic relationships to grow personally and professionally within groups. Broken relationships lead to group dysfunctions. Humans are already imperfect, and as a group grows in complexity, the number of imperfections within the group increases. These imperfections create faults and gaps in productivity between individuals. Healing facilitates improvements in the emotional components of the dyadic relationships within a group.

Successful leaders view organizations' ills as requiring healing, not removal or change. Healing in this context is an extension of learning. This is an application or action of a leader's empathy—caring enough for the people you interact with to recognize their needs and focus energy on solving them. The healing focuses on the first-aid approach rather than a destructive rip-and-repair solution. You cannot heal what you remove or destroy. Leaders who focus on healing themselves and others through education and training will benefit from the growth in productivity and loyalty. All humans share a desire for healing as it makes them whole.

A typical leader views themselves as something other than a healer, but an inclusive leader makes others whole by focusing on a larger purpose than themselves. Leaders who act on empathy, compassion, and healing by teaching build an effective and sustainable workforce. A leader can heal followers through counseling, knowledge, and a positive example. The targeted followers react with a sense of cohesiveness and collaboration, leading to in-groups. Recovery helps establish an emotional and operational balance that allows creativity and change. Many people rely on their emotions and translate them into reality and their version of the facts.

Studies in several different contexts have shown that creating positive cultures will facilitate positive organizational behaviors and higher performance. Focusing on the emotional state of followers within the spirit of healing can help focus knowledge and provide motivation for action. At some point, a leader must focus on the perceptions and actions required to alleviate the cause of negative dyadic relationships. Healing through education is a means to facilitate a positive dyadic relationship between members of an organization.

A broken person or organization is stagnant, with most free energy going into the problem. Organizations and people must learn through healing to move forward.

Chapter Seven

———— ∾∾∾ ————

COMMUNICATION

HARNESSING THE ABILITY to communicate effectively is a leader's most important skill. Most perspectives on communication revolve around sending information, translations, and receiver reactions. Effective communication is established when the intended audience understands and acts on the intended message. It is a set of planned and unplanned actions that influence others.

Communication is more than a simple tool for leadership; it is the core component of every dyadic relationship. A typical leadership approach to communications focuses on it as a means or mechanism required to gain the desired results. However, an increasing number of viewpoints leverage communication as a broader way to influence dyadic relationships directly and indirectly in an organization.

Leadership communications should be more than the one-way messaging commonly found in organizations. The impact that communication has on dyadic relationships is too complex for anyone to understand fully. Leaders need to realize that the message received is not controlled by them directly but due to the dyadic interactions between them and their followers, which means communication is a culmination of actions and exchanges, not a single event. All of your interactions inform others and are part of your communication process. The leader spends more than half of their day on communications. As a result, many organizations perceive moving information or communications as a critical element of success for any potential leader.

Listening is hearing and receiving what is said and unsaid. Inclusive leadership requires a deep commitment to listening to others and that internal voice to understand followers and dyadic relationships. This learned discipline makes a leader and followers receptive to others and facilitates acknowledging others' perspectives and viewpoints.

It takes effort from leaders and followers to listen. A practical application of listening requires an interest in what others are communicating and seeking clarification from those sharing the information. The perception of being an attentive listener is just as important as receiving and understanding the message sent. This perception and having the ability to receive give closure to those sending information. A leader cannot be effective without effective communication. There is a need to be a skilled communicator in countless relationships at the organizational level to achieve results through others.

BIAS

As a leader who wants to create an inclusive environment, you must think clearly, express ideas, and share information with many audiences. It would help if you learned to handle the rapid flow of information within the organization and with your stakeholders and influencers. A leader needs to know how and when to communicate. This is one of those topics in most management training or academic courses.

Communication is similar to a relationship. You may have a perception that does not align with reality or how others in the relationship perceive it. There are many influences on communications, and bias is significant.

A listening bias results from hearing what is exciting or perceived meaning and not the intended message. This bias is one of the factors in followers' group formation. It is a factor that influences what group a person will find comfortable. Bias can form when the prevalent desires of either party are not in line with expectations or perceptions. Suppose a leader is not perceived as caring about a specific group of followers. In that case, followers will naturally form a subgroup, eventually leading to an out-group status. Recognizing bias and establishing a connection between leaders and followers will nudge followers into in-groups. This is done by genuinely caring for others and developing a personal and emotional connection with one's dyadic relationships. Care and communicate toward success.

DIRECTION

Communication is the means of articulating the direction for success. In the example of the Marine, having an expected and known result to any basic command is founded on the understanding that the follower's intent is known, articulated, and received for action. The Marines developed tools, training, and cultural norms to ensure good communication.

Every Marine has the information needed to complete or know the expected result for every event they are engaged in. The intent of the communication is easier to understand when the context is well-defined. A typical organization can leverage its vision as that baseline understanding. If a leader has a well-defined vision and only communicates and moves the organization to meet that vision, the intent of the communication is easier to understand. The context is clear, and the intent is known or easily recognizable.

The Marine Corps uses many tools to ensure communication is articulated. Some forms of communication have a predefined format. For example, they have a standard format for issuing organizational directions known as the five-paragraph order. Suppose a junior Marine leader hears they have a five-paragraph order on the way. In that case, they immediately know they have a mission assigned to them. This helps communicate a combat action clearly and concisely by a known format for the thorough orientation of the area of operations. Other organizations can use forms, reports, statements, and other standardized documents to help provide context to the information communicated.

There are other tools that help ensure the communication is adequately articulated, from standardized language to expected norms. A well-known example is the communication of the time. The average person would communicate time using numbers, possibly an early (AM) or late day (PM) modifier with a time zone. A problem can arise when time is provided to someone in a different time zone or without knowing the context. The communicator only gives a number; everything is assumed as known. The military solves this by using a twenty-four-hour clock and a predefined referenced time zone. So, a person on a Pacific Island can hear the 1920 Zulu and know the exact time for them. Suppose they hear 7:20 as the time for the event. They need more data to ensure the context is known from morning or evening to the time zone. There are other tools, from using a standard phonetic alphabet to hand signals. Marines use these tools to reduce the opportunity for confusion and a loss of the ability to articulate data properly. Other organizations use acronyms, symbols, and shortcuts to make communications faster and ensure only the correct data is transmitted.

Effective communication also needs the receiver to translate the data received into the desired information and act on it. The Marine Corps uses a simple acknowledgment tool to help ensure this critical step in the communication process works. Every military-style basic training includes having a trainer ask the recruit or student simple questions in a loud, confusing, and noisy environment. The students or recruits are expected to immediately respond with a simple repeatable phrase from "sir, yes, sir" to "yes, drill sergeant" or another acceptable norm. Some people view this tactic as cruel or a sick form of entertainment. In reality, the instructors establish the standards early, even in the most stressful situations, that every received and understood order requires acknowledgment. This final component is critical in the Marines's highly dynamic and stressful environments. As a leader, knowing your communication is in a known format, language, and context and was received for action ensures you are effectively communicating.

Many leaders and organizations do not have the acknowledgment step as a policy or continual practice and likely have some communication issues. Everyone does not need to yell down the hall after a meeting, text, email, or note indicating a new task or piece of data. There should be an acceptable norm of "OK" from a task or data exchange. There can even be language shortcuts like a response of "K" from everyone on the "to" line of a message to the message indicating no response is required. As a leader, you should have acceptable norms relating to communication responses. Communication is the foundational component of the dyadic relationship. An organization cannot move faster than it can communicate.

Chapter Eight

———❦———

ACTION

ACTION IN THIS context is the idea of movement portrayed by positive persuasion. Persuasion is a process of communication used to influence others. This is built on the idea that having a convincing argument is better than a simple directive. Having followers agree with the direction will provide a better environment.

Inclusive leadership relies on persuasion over traditional positional authority. An authoritarian style is like leaders who believe that micromanagement and other leadership techniques are effective. The conventional authoritarian style of directing others into action does not work well in an inclusive environment in the modern era.

Leadership that shares knowledge and understanding of the situation while building a consensus develops an inclusive workforce that facilitates in-group development. Having that inclusive workforce is a requirement for making a significant in-group presence. One can influence by moving from a coercion-type approach to leadership toward convincing and guidance. The end goal of persuasion is to move an organization forward. It takes movement for change. Movement, along with continual improvement, creates a positive performance environment.

Followers must be willing to cooperate, or the best-laid plans will fail. In the Marine example, the Field Day was completed on time because the followers agreed to put in the effort. There was no large meeting before the event, a well-planned paper schedule, or a list of activities. Everyone had a complete understanding of what was needed, with a shared understanding of what was required, and did it. The junior leaders did not need to yell or articulate a detailed plan. They covered the expected overall objective in a conversation format. They allowed the followers to ask clarification questions and volunteer for roles they felt comfortable doing.

CYCLE

The best way to create, maintain, or improve any environment or relationship is with an approach that provides continual improvements. Continuous improvement is the quest to improve. A continuous improvement cycle is portrayed in the form of a circle, showing that the concept of improvement is never completed. This never-ending activity is full of change and movement. There are many variations of this concept in use. These are the Deming wheel, the Shewhart cycle, the Kaizen approach, The Toyota Way, PDCA (Plan-Do-Check-Act), OPDCA (Observe-Plan-Do-Check-Act), and others—iterative design and management methodologies used in business, engineering, and leadership fields to manage continuous improvements. The critical point of all these processes is that they are not a quick fix to any problem, including a broken dyadic relationship between the leader and followers. Applying these scientific processes to create an inclusive environment or improve the dyadic relationship will work over time.

APPLICATION

Positive leadership in action is more than the surface goal of completing a task. The Marines of Building 1620 completed the work required while training and supporting each other. In some ways, they worked as a single in-group. They understood it requires action or movement to meet their goals and had a shared vision of the task at hand. Most of the required activities were completed as an instinctive act of community support. The direction, timeline, and vision were based on a weekly task and a well-known test at the end.

The building members are part of a fraternity that will last longer than the time spent on active duty. Even now, they are still a family, and from spirit and policy, once a Marine, they are always Marines. Ultimately, some Marines in that building were not part of the in-group. They did not last long in the Corps, and one of them lost an internal struggle with suicide. The failed relationships lasted for their entire lives and, in some cases, changed their destiny. The great leaders from that group learned to serve others over themselves. They understood that those who desire to be great must help others, and the great came not to be served but to serve others first. What was not known was the impact leaders have on followers based on the quality of their dyadic interactions.

When an inclusive organization moves toward success, there is leadership. Leadership happens when you move.

THE LEADERSHIP THEORY

My journey with the servant leadership theory started with the 1957 edition of the Hermann Hesse novel The Journey to the East, translated by Hilda Rosner. It was not the most straightforward book to read, and it did take some time to understand the story. I then read the 1977 text by Robert Greenleaf on servant leadership, all before doing the scholarly research required within my doctoral program. When I first started the research on servant leadership, I had this concern. My initial interpretation of the text and what I understood about servant leadership did not always match the accepted steps, elements, and principles provided within the research community. I decided to take an approach to the text that would help me find the critical explanation or interpretation of the text to help my understanding of the topic. I did an extensive exegesis exercise that became an extensive mind map. I was able to distill that down to ten basic tenets. I printed them on paper and put them on the wall next to my desk. To my surprise, you can find some components of those in every scholarly and contemporary work I found associated with the topic of Servant Leadership.

Servant leadership is a leadership philosophy that emphasizes the role of leaders as servants first. How this happens and manifests itself is different in every single application. It does not mean there is no focus on organizational goals, objectives, and measurements toward success, and this is not the chickens running the chicken coup theory. My application is about being successful while serving others to help them grow, develop, and achieve their full potential. I see a servant leader as one who operates from a mindset of empathy, humility, and a genuine desire to support the people they lead. They foster an environment of trust, collaboration, and mutual respect. This creates an inclusive environment with diverse ideas, concepts, and perceptions and a focus on meeting the organization's goals and objectives.

My mind map exercise resulted in listening, empathy, awareness, conceptualization, foresight, stewardship, persuasion, healing, building a community, and a commitment to growth. These ten tenets are categorized into the five characteristics of vision, care, learning, communication, and action.

REFLECTIONS

ONE

1. Can you identify the three leadership rules in this text?
   Do you agree with them?
2. There are several leadership "challenges" with no resolution.
   What is your resolution to these challenges? Have you seen or had
   a challenge with a similar solution?
3. Have you been in a situation where the initial reaction or option
   you wanted to employ to solve a problem was unavailable? How
   long did it take to get to the next option, and did it work?
4. Is there an overarching leadership theme that stands out in this text?
5. Can you identify a leadership definition or theory within this text?

TWO

6. What is a dyad and why is it essential?
7. Followers can form groups among themselves within a larger organization. Can you identify the two main groups?

8. Have you been in a situation where you can now recognize the formation of groups?
9. Does an overarching leadership theme stand out in this text?
10. Can you identify a leadership definition or theory within this text?

THREE

11. Can you explain the characteristics and tenets of an inclusive leadership approach?
12. Have you seen or used any components of an inclusive leadership approach?
13. Is there a component of the approach you think is missing?
14. Does an overarching leadership theme stand out in this text?
15. Can you identify a leadership definition or theory within this text?

FOUR

16. What is your perspective on 360-degree and other performance evaluation methods?
17. What is your impression of the inclusive leadership approach?
18. Are cultural considerations required to apply this approach to leadership?

Thank You

Find me on social media, subscribe, and communicate. We all learn and grow from our engagements with others. There are no limits to positive dyads.

<u>Please provide your comments and review of this book with your favorite bookstore and review sites of choice.</u>

Jim

The universal definition of leadership

Leadership is the act of influencing, resulting in a difference, causing a change measured by movement.

BIBLIOGRAPHY

Ahlstrand, Amanda L., Laurie J. Bassi, and Daniel P. McMurrer. 2003. "Workplace Education for Low-Wage Workers." Kalamazoo, Mich: W.E. Upjohn Institute for Employment Research.

Albinsson, Pia A. and B. Yasanthi Perera. 2012. "Alternative Marketplaces in the 21st Century: Building Community Through Sharing Events," Journal of Consumer Behaviour 11, 11, no. 4: 303–15.

Arsovski, Slavko and Srđan Nikezić. 2012. "Leadership Communications and Quality."

Atwijuka, Sylvia and Cam Caldwell. 2017. "Authentic Leadership and the Ethic of Care," The Journal of Management Development 36, 36, no. 8: 1040–51.

Barbuto, John E. and Daniel W. Wheeler. 2006. "Scale Development and Construct Clarification of Servant Leadership," Group & Organization Management 31, 31, no. 3: 300–326.

Basile, F. 1996. "Great Management Ideas Can Work for You," Indianapolis Business Journal 16, 16, no. 1: 53–54.

Baty, Wayne. 1968. "Book Reviews: Communication and Communication Systems," Lee O. Thayer, Richard D. Irwin, Inc., Homewood, Illinois, 1968, 375 Pages." Journal of Business Communication 5. Thousand Oaks, CA: Sage Publications.

Bertland, Alexander. 2012. "The Limits of Workplace Community: Jean-Luc Nancy and the Possibility of Teambuilding." Edited by Patrick Flanagan, Marilynn Fleckenstein, Victoria Shoaf, and Patricia Werhane, Journal of Business Ethics 99, 99, no. Suppl 1: 1–8.

Boyes-Watson, Carolyn. 2005. "Community Is Not a Place but a Relationship: Lessons for Organizational Development," Public Organization Review 5, 5, no. 4: 359–74.

Breunig, Mary. 2005. "Turning Experiential Education and Critical Pedagogy Theory into Praxis," The Journal of Experiential Education 28, 28, no. 2: 106–22.

Canevello, Amy and Jennifer Crocker. 2010. "Creating Good Relationships: Responsiveness, Relationship Quality, and Interpersonal Goals." Edited by Jeffrey Simpson, Journal of Personality and Social Psychology 99, 99, no. 1: 78–106.

Caporael, Linnda R. 1997. "The Evolution of Truly Social Cognition: The Core Configurations Model," Personality and Social Psychology Review 1, 1, no. 4: 276–98.

Castilho, Marcelo and Carlos Quandt. 2017. "Collaborative Capability in Coworking Spaces: Convenience Sharing or Community Building?" Technology Innovation Management Review 7, 7, no. 12: 32–42. https://doi.org/10.22215/timreview/1126.

Chassie, Marilyn Bache, Bsn, and Management Science. 1984. "Vertical Dyadic Linkage Formation: Predictors and Processes Determining Quality Superior-Subordinate Relationships."

Claar, Victor V., Lonnie L. Jackson, and Vicki R. Tenhaken. 2014. "Are Servant Leaders Born or Made?" SLTP 1.

Cornish, Edward. 2004. *Futuring: The Exploration of the Future.* World Future Society.

Craft, Ralph C. and Charles Leake. 2002. "The Pareto Principle in Organizational Decision Making," Management Decision 40, 40, no. 8: 729–33.

Dahl, Allison, Jill Lawrence, and Jeff Pierce. 2011. "Building An Innovation Community," Research Technology Management 54, 54, no. 5: 19–27.

Dansereau, Fred, James Cashman, and George Graen. 1973. "Instrumentality Theory and Equity Theory as Complementary Approaches in Predicting the Relationship of Leadership and Turnover among Managers," Organizational Behavior and Human Performance 10, 10, no. 2: 184–200.

Dansereau, Fred, George Bear Graen, and William J. Haga. 1975. "A Vertical Dyad Linkage Approach to Leadership within Formal Organizations: A Longitudinal Investigation of the Role Making Process," Organizational Behavior and Human Performance 13, 13, no. 1: 46.

Davenport, Brian. 2015. "Compassion, Suffering and Servant-Leadership: Combining Compassion and Servant-Leadership to Respond to Suffering," Leadership 11, 11, no. 3: 300–315.

Davis, James H., F. David Schoorman, and Lex Donaldson. 1997. "Toward a Stewardship Theory of Management," The Academy of Management Review 22, 22, no. 1: 20–47.

Drucker, Peter F. 2018. *The Effective Executive*. Routledge.

Eddleston, Kimberly A. and Franz W. Kellermanns. 2007. "Destructive and Productive Family Relationships: A Stewardship Theory Perspective," Journal of Business Venturing 22, 22, no. 4: 545–65.

Ehrhart, Mark G., Paul Hanges, Keith Hattrup, Katherine Klein, Robert Ployhart, Cynthia Stevens, Paul Tesluk, and Karen Holcombe. n.d. "Leadership and Procedural Justice Climate Citizenship Behavior As Antecedents of Unit-Level Organizational Citizenship Behavior," Personnel Psychology 200. 57.61-94.

Ezerman, Maria Marina and Desak Ketut Sintaasih. 2018. "Effect of Servant Leadership, Trust in Leadership on Organizational Citizenship Behavior with Interpersonal Communications as Mediation Variables," IOSR Journal of Business and Management, 20 (4), 21–30.

Fremlin, J. 2015. "Identifying Concepts That Build a Sense of Community in a Mediated World."

Gardner, J. W. 1991. *Building community*. Washington, DC: Independent Sector.

Gedney, Christine R, Maxwell Air Force Base, and Alabama. 1999. "Leadership Effectiveness and Gender." Defense Technical Information Center.

Gerber, Christine. 2021. "Community Building on Crowdwork Platforms: Autonomy and Control of Online Workers?" Edited by

Gale Raj-Reichert, Nicole Helmerich, and Sabrina Zajak, Competition & Change 25, 25, no. 2: 190–211.

Graen, George B. and Mary Uhl-Bien. 1995. "Relationship-Based Approach to Leadership: Development of Leader-Member Exchange (LMX) Theory of Leadership over 25 Years: Applying a Multi-Level Multi-Domain Perspective," The Leadership Quarterly 6, 6, no. 2: 219–47.

Greenleaf, Robert K. 1977. *Servant Leadership: A Journey into the Nature of Legitimate Power and Greatness.* New York: Paulist Press.

Greenleaf, Robert K. 2002. *Servant Leadership: A Journey into the Nature of Legitimate Power and Greatness.* 25 Anniversary Edition. Paulist Press.

Gross-Schaefer, Arthur, Jeff Trigilio, Jamie Negus, and Ceng-Si Ro. 2000. "Ethics Education in the Workplace: An Effective Tool to Combat Employee Theft," Journal of Business Ethics 26, 26, no. 2: 89–100.

Hall, Stephen S. 2011. *Wisdom: From Philosophy to Neuroscience.* Vintage.

Hastorf, Albert H. and Hadley Cantril. 1954. "They Saw a Game; a Case Study," The Journal of Abnormal and Social Psychology 49, 49, no. 1: 129.

Hazy, James K. and Mary Uhl-Bien. 2015. "Towards Operationalizing Complexity Leadership: How Generative, Administrative and Community-Building Leadership Practices Enact Organizational Outcomes," Leadership (London, England) 11, 11, no. 1: 79–104.

Hesse, Hermann. 1957. The journey to the East. New York. The Noonday Press, Inc.

Hines, Andy. 2006. "Strategic Foresight: The State of the Art," The Futurist 40, 40, no. 5: 18.

Hogg, Michael A., Daan van Knippenberg, and David E. Rast. 2012. "The Social Identity Theory of Leadership: Theoretical Origins, Research Findings, and Conceptual Developments," European Review of Social Psychology 23, 23, no. 1: 258–304.

Hogg, Michael A., Robin Martin, Olga Epitropaki, Aditi Mankad, Alicia Svensson, and Karen Weeden. 2005. "Effective Leadership in Salient Groups: Revisiting Leader-Member Exchange Theory From the Perspective of the Social Identity Theory of Leadership," Personality & Social Psychology bulletin 31, 31, no. 7: 991–1004.

Jit, Ravinder, C. S. Sharma, and Mona Kawatra. 2017. "Healing a Broken Spirit: Role of Servant Leadership," Vikalpa 42, 42, no. 2: 80–94.

Johnson, Scott D. and Curt Bechler. 1998. "Examining the Relationship Between Listening Effectiveness and Leadership Emergence: Perceptions, Behaviors, and Recall," Small Group Research 29, 29, no. 4: 452–71.

Kakabadse, Nada, Andrew Kakabadse, and Linda Lee-Davies. 2005. "Visioning the Pathway: A Leadership Process Model," European Management Journal 23, 23, no. 2: 237–46.

Kong, Dongmin, Bohui Zhang, and Jian Zhang. 2022. "Higher Education and Corporate Innovation," Journal of Corporate Finance 72, 72: 102165.

Laub, James. 1999. "Assessing the Servant Organization of the Servant Organizational Assessment (SOLA) Instrument. Leveraging the Power of Servant Leadership." Cham: Springer International Publishing.

Lee, Bill. 2013. "The Power of Peer Influence: Traditional Marketing Is on Its Way Out. In Its Place, America's Most Innovative Companies Are Implementing New, More Authentic Techniques Based on Peer Influence and Community Building," ABA Bank Marketing 45, 45, no. 6: 24.

Lejeune, John A. 1922. "Kindly and Just." Marine Corps University. Washington, DC. https://www.usmcu.edu/Research/Marine-Corps-History-Division/Frequently-Requested-Topics/Historical-Documents-Orders-and-Speeches/Kindly-and-Just/.

Liden, R. C. and G. Graen. 1980. "Generalizability of the Vertical Dyad Linkage Model of Leadership," Academy of Management Journal 23, 23, no. 3: 451–65.

Liden, Robert C. and John M. Maslyn. 1998. "Multidimensionality of Leader-Member Exchange: An Empirical Assessment Through Scale Development," Journal of Management 24, 24, no. 1: 43–72.

Liden, Robert C., Sandy J. Wayne, Hao Zhao, and David Henderson. 2008. "Servant Leadership: Development of a Multidimensional Measure and Multi-Level Assessment," The Leadership Quarterly 19, 19, no. 2: 161–77.

Malcolm, Susan B. and Nell Tabor Hartley. 2010. "Chester Barnard's Moral Persuasion, Authenticity, and Trust: Foundations for Leadership." Edited by Joyce Heames, Journal of Management History 16, 16, no. 4: 454–67.

Manz, Charles C. and Henry P. Sims Jr. 1987. "Leading Workers to Lead Themselves: The External Leadership of Self-Managing Work Teams," Administrative Science Quarterly, 106–29.

Marsh, Nick, Mike McAllum, and Dominique Purcell. 2002. *Strategic Foresight: The Power of Standing in the Future*. Crown Content.

McMinn Jr, Thomas Franklin. 2001. "The Conceptualization and Perception of Biblical Servant Leadership in the Southern Baptist Convention." The Southern Baptist Theological Seminary.

Millett, Stephen M. 2006. "Futuring and Visioning: Complementary Approaches to Strategic Decision Making," Strategy & Leadership 34, 34, no. 3: 43–50.

Molenberghs, Pascal. 2013. "The Neuroscience of In-Group Bias," Neuroscience and Biobehavioral Reviews 37, 37, no. 8: 1530–36.

Nirenberg, John. 1994. "From Team Building to Community Building," Global Business and Organizational Excellence 14, 14, no. 1: 51.

Northouse, Peter Guy. 2022. *Leadership: Theory and Practice*. Thousand Oaks: SAGE.

O'Connell, Dave, Karl Hickerson, and Arun Pillutla. 2011. "Organizational Visioning: An Integrative Review," Group & Organization Management 36, 36, no. 1: 103–25.

Oechsli, Matt. 2021. "How to Overcome the Human Listening Bias Trap," Wealth Management, https://ezproxy.regent.edu/login?url=https://www.proquest.com/trade-journals/how-overcome-human-listening-bias-trap/docview/2488087751/se-2?accountid=13479.

Page, Don and T. Paul Wong. 2000. "A Conceptual Framework for Measuring Servant Leadership," *The Human Factor in Shaping the Course of History and Development* 69, 69: 110.

Patriarche, Crystal. 2009. "Teaching Kids to Help Others." SheKnows. Penske Media Corporation.

Peck, Richard. 2017. "How to Create a Culture of Giving in Your Business: Your Company Can Do Good AND Do Well—While Supporting Critical Services, Strengthening Communities and Building Team Camaraderie," New Hampshire Business Review 39, 39, no. 23: A8.

Ruben, Brent D. and Ralph A. Gigliotti. 2016a. "Leadership as Social Influence: An Expanded View of Leadership Communication Theory and Practice," Journal of Leadership & Organizational Studies 23, 23, no. 4: 467–79.

Ruben, Brent D. and Ralph A. Gigliotti. 2016b. "Leadership as Social Influence: An Expanded View of Leadership Communication Theory and Practice," Journal of Leadership & Organizational Studies 23, 23, no. 4: 467–79.

Russell, Robert F. and A. Gregory Stone. 2002. "A Review of Servant Leadership Attributes: Developing a Practical Model," Leadership & Organization Development Journal 23, 23, no. 3: 145–57.

Sendjaya, Sen, James C. Sarros, and Joseph C. Santora. 2008. "Defining and Measuring Servant Leadership Behaviour in Organizations," Journal of Management Studies 45, 45, no. 2: 402–24.

Showry, Mendemu and KVL Manasa. 2014. "Self-Awareness—Key to Effective Leadership," IUP Journal of Soft Skills 8, 8, no. 1.

Sinek, Simon. 2014. *Leaders Eat Last: Why Some Teams Pull Together and Others Don't*. Penguin.

Smith, Brien N., Ray V. Montagno, and Tatiana N. Kuzmenko. 2004. "Transformational and Servant Leadership: Content and Contextual Comparisons," The Journal of Leadership Studies 10, 10, no. 4: 80–91.

Song, Jiying. 2018a. "Leading Through Awareness and Healing: A Servant-Leadership Model," The International Journal of Servant-Leadership 12, 12, no. 1: 245–84.

Sosik, John J. and Shelley D. Dionne. 1997. "Leadership Styles and Deming's Behavior Factors," Journal of Business and Psychology 11, 11, no. 4: 447–62.

Spears, Larry C. 1995. *Reflections on Leadership: How Robert K. Greenleaf's Theory of Servant-Leadership Influenced Today's Top Management Thinkers*. Wiley.

Spears, Larry C. 1998. *Insights on Leadership: Service, Stewardship, Spirit, and Servant-Leadership*. New York, Wiley.

Spears, Larry C. 2010. "Character and Servant Leadership: Ten Characteristics of Effective, Caring Leaders," The Journal of Virtues & Leadership 1, 1, no. 1: 25–30.

Steffens, Niklas K., Nathan Wolyniec, Tyler G. Okimoto, Frank Mols, S. Alexander Haslam, and Adam A. Kay. 2021. "Knowing Me, Knowing Us: Personal and Collective Self-Awareness Enhances Authentic Leadership and Leader Endorsement," The Leadership Quarterly 32, 32, no. 6: 101498.

Sutrisno, Timotius F. C. W. and Elia Ardyan. 2020. "Achieving Organizational Performance in Food Companies: The Critical Role of

Leadership and Continuous Improvement as Part of TQM Practice," Calitatea 21, 21, no. 177: 133–38.

Tafvelin, Susanne, Henna Hasson, Stefan Holmström, and Ulrica von Thiele Schwarz. 2019. "Are Formal Leaders the Only Ones Benefitting From Leadership Training? A Shared Leadership Perspective," Journal of Leadership & Organizational Studies 26, 26, no. 1: 32–43.

Tajfel, Henri, M. G. Billig, R. P. Bundy, and Claude Flament. 1971. "Social Categorization and Intergroup Behaviour," European Journal of Social Psychology 1, 1, no. 2: 149–78.

Thrasher, Gregory. 2020. "Social Identity Theory and Leader-Member Exchange." Organization Management Journal 17. Emerald.

Turner, John C., Penelope J. Oakes, S Alexander Haslam, and Craig McGarty. 1994. "Self and Collective: Cognition and Social Context," Personality and Social Psychology Bulletin 20, 20, no. 5: 454–63.

Venus, Merlijn, Daan Stam, and Daan Van Knippenberg. 2019. "Visions of Change as Visions of Continuity," Academy of Management Journal 62, 62, no. 3: 667–90.

Wallace, Stein W. 2000. "Decision Making Under Uncertainty: Is Sensitivity Analysis of Any Use?" Operations Research 48, 48, no. 1: 20–25.

Wang, Lei, Meng-Yu Cheng, and Song Wang. 2018. "Carrot or Stick? The Role of In-Group/Out-Group on the Multilevel Relationship Between Authoritarian and Differential Leadership and Employee Turnover Intention," Journal of Business Ethics 152, 152, no. 4: 1069–84.

Weymes, Ed. 2002. "Relationships Not Leadership Sustain Successful Organisations," Journal of Change Management 3, 3, no. 4: 319–31.

Wheeler, Daniel W. 2012. *Servant Leadership for Higher Education: Principles and Practices*. San Francisco, Calif: Jossey-Bass, Wiley, John Wiley & Sons, Incorporated.

Yamagishi, Toshio, Nobuhito Jin, and Allan S. Miller. 1998. "In-Group Bias and Culture of Collectivism," Asian Journal of Social Psychology 1, 1, no. 3: 315–28.

Zander, Thea, Michael Öllinger, and Kirsten G. Volz. 2016. "Intuition and Insight: Two Processes That Build on Each Other or Fundamentally Differ?" Frontiers in Psychology 7, 7: 1395.

Zhang, Zhonglu, Yi Lei, and Hong Li. 2016. "Approaching the Distinction between Intuition and Insight," Frontiers in Psychology 7, 7: 1195.

GLY Group

A leading-edge provider of leadership, strategic foresight, planning, and engagement information and materials.

www.glygroup.net
info@glygroup.net

God is Love

www.ingramcontent.com/pod-product-compliance
Lightning Source LLC
Chambersburg PA
CBHW052101270326
41931CB00012B/2845